6 00 158741 8   TELEPEN

KU-615-707

An Annotated Bibliography
of
John Updike Criticism
1967-1973,
and A Checklist of His Works

BRITISH LIBRARY
LENDING DIVISION

-9 NOV 1978

Y 3/7353

An Annotated Bibliography
of
John Updike Criticism
1967-1973,
and A Checklist of His Works

Michael A. Olivas

WITHDRAWN

Garland Publishing, Inc., New York & London

1975

Copyright © 1975
by Michael A. Olivas
All Rights Reserved

The British Library

Discarded from the
Reference Division

Library of Congress Cataloging in Publication Data

Olivas, Michael A
   An annotated bibliography of John Updike criticism,
1967-1973, and a checklist of his works.

   1. Updike, John--Bibliography. I. Title.
Z8913.85.04   016.813'5'4   74-13951
ISBN 0-8240-1053-1

Printed in the United States of America

Contents

Introduction

Annotated bibliography for the works of John Updike is complete through July, 1967; the subsequent publication of *Couples, Bech: A Book,* and *Rabbit Redux* has necessitated a revision of this collation. *Couples* in particular generated much criticism, heralded by a *Time* cover story and fanfare over the movie rights. But while Updike's reputation has grown, bibliographical scholarship has not progressed. A 1970 "Compleat Updike" was published, in three editions, yet no major revision of the original checklist has been attempted. The Spring, 1974 *Modern Fiction Studies* will be devoted to Updike and will undoubtedly create further interest in the author. The purpose of this book is to provide both the necessary annotated bibliography of criticism on Updike and the checklist of his complete works, collected and uncollected. The list is compiled through January, 1974 and subsequent entries are noted intermittently through June, 1974.

This bibliography, then, is designed to supplement *John Updike: A Bibliography* by C. Clarke Taylor (Kent, Ohio: Kent State University Press, 1968) in style and critical approach. I have utilized the general chapter headings and subdivisions of this Serif Bibliography and have recorded information in a manner consistent with the original list. Hopefully, this will facilitate the eventual revision of my bibliography by me or someone else assembling a complete list of Updike criticism. I have attempted to annotate each entry accurately and thoroughly in the list and have noted the sources of entries not seen by me. In most cases, the source was Edward P. Vargo's *Rainstorms and Fire: Ritual in the Novels of John Updike* (Port Washington, New York:

INTRODUCTION

Kennikat Press, 1973) or indexes like the *Modern Language Association Annual Bibliography* (*MLA*) or *Abstracts of English Studies* (*AES*). The annotations are descriptive rather than evaluative, in almost all instances. Exceptions are made to note an entry as particularly helpful or less than helpful. I frequently quote portions of articles to give a sense of author's tone and style.

The editorial style is intentially similar to Taylor's. Likewise, variations from his techniques are not capricious. The numbers employed in the 1968 Serif text serve only to show how much Updike has written since, so I have not numbered my entries. However, a future compiler could combine the two texts with little difficulty. Perhaps the most dramatic difference is in the listing of secondary sources. Taylor could list only nine books which had chapters on Updike; my list contains more than this which are full-length volumes on the author. In fact, criticism has increased dramatically: articles have become chapters in books; dissertations have been published as articles and full-length books; reviews and review-essays have proliferated. Most importantly, Updike continues to be widely published. I have retained Taylor's division between book and journal/periodical. Since more critics have begun to judge Updike's oeuvre in its entirety, the distinction drawn by Taylor between articles and reviews seem quaint. I have chosen to combine articles and reviews and instead distinguish between general and specific articles on Updike's works. This seems more realistic in terms of mounting numbers of critical judgments on his fiction. Since Updike is reprinted in several languages, he draws much critical attention in foreign journals. However, like Taylor, I have chosen to include primarily criticism in English. Exceptions to this are foreign entries in standard indexes and sources available to me. Unlike Taylor, I did not choose to note the original sources of collected material by Updike. Since the reprinted, collected volumes all remain in print, they are more accessible than a given issue of a journal or magazine. For this reason I listed the contents of collections of stories and essays and noted the original sources of those pieces not reprinted by Updike. My underlying editorial rationale was consistency with Taylor's volume, accuracy, and thoroughness.

The sheer quantity of material does not guarantee its availability. Nor does one ever exhaust the possible sources of information. In fact, serendipity was as much a factor in this compilation as was having access to a large research library. My basic bibliographic tool was Richard Altick and Andrew Wright, comps. *Selective Biliography for the Study of English and American Literature* (New York: Macmillan, 1971) and its sources. However, these sources did not exhaust all possibilities. Colleagues have put me on to pieces; publishers' flyers have notified me of sources; footnotes in articles have clued me still further. Although I acknowledge these sources, full blame for errors must be mine.

Columbus, Ohio
March, 1974

I owe thanks to many persons, particularly Professors Richard Weatherford, Chris Zacher, and Dan Barnes of the Ohio State University. For tracking down books and helping me with many library matters, these persons deserve my acknowledgment: Helen Wada, Thurber Room, Ohio State University; Professor Zeph Steward, Lowell House, Harvard; William Bond, Houghton Librarian, Harvard; Jeanne Broburg, Woodbury Room, Lamont, Harvard; Mary Gerard, Patterson Room, University of Lousiville; Mrs. Cawley and the kind ladies at the Ipswich Public Library; Elizabeth Newton, Ipswich Historical Society; the personnel at Houghton, Harvard and the Rare Book Room, Library of Congress;

INTRODUCTION

Barbara Langenberger, *New York Times*; Linda Hertz, *Scientific American*; Martha McGill, Alfred A. Knopf Co.; Ruth Rogin, the *New Yorker*. Special acknowledgment is due John Updike, who has courteously allowed me to photocopy many of his works, and who has been very accommodating in answering my tedious questions. I dedicate this book to him and my wife, Thelma. John Updike gave me the reason for this book; she gave me the courage to complete it.

A. PRIMARY SOURCES

1. Books

Novels

The Poorhouse Fair. New York: Knopf, 1959.

Rabbit, Run. New York: Knopf, 1960. Revised and reprinted

with The Poorhouse Fair. New York: Modern Library, 1965.

The Centaur. New York: Knopf, 1963.

Of the Farm. New York: Knopf, 1965.

Couples. New York: Knopf, 1968.

Rabbit Redux. New York: 1971.

Short Stories

The Same Door. New York: Knopf, 1959. Contents: "Friends
from Philadelphia"; "Ace in the Hole"; "Tomorrow and Tomorrow
and So Forth"; "Dentristry and Doubt"; "The Kid's Whistling";
"Toward Evening"; "Snowing in Greenwich Village"; "Who Made
Yellow Roses Yellow?"; "Sunday Teasing"; "His Finest Hour";
"A Trillion Feed of Gas"; "Incest"; "A Gift From the City";
"Intercession"; "The Alligators"; "The Happiest I've Been."

Pigeon Feathers and Other Stories. New York: Knopf, 1962.
Contents: "Walter Briggs"; "The Persistence of Desire";
"Still Life"; "Flight"; "Should Wizard Hit Mommy?"' "A
Sense of Shelter"; "Dear Alexandros"; "Wife-Wooing"; "Pigeon
Feather"; "Home"; "Archangel"; "You'll Never Know, Dear, How
Much I Love You"; "The Astronomer"; "A & P"; The Doctor's
Wife"; "Lifeguard"; "The Crow in the Woods"; "The Blessed
Man of Boston, My Grandmother's Thimble, and Fanning Island";
"Packed Dirt, Churchgoing, A Dying Cat, A Traded Car."

Olinger Stories. New York: Vintage, 1964. Contents: "Forward."
You'll Never Know, Dear, How Much I Love You"; "The
Alligators"; "Pigeon Feathers"; "Friends From Philadelphia";
"Flight"; "A Sense of Shelter"; "The Happiest I've Been";
"The Persistence of Desire"; "The Blessed Man of Boston, My
Grandmother's Thimble, and Fanning Island"; "Packed Dirt,
Churchgoing, A Dying Cat, A Traded Car"; "In Football Season."

The Music School. New York: Knopf, 1966. Contents: "In Football Season"; "The Indian"; "Giving Blood"; "A Madman"; "Leaves"; "The Stare"; "Avec La Bebe-sitter"; "Twin Beds in Rome"; "Four Sides of One Story"; "The Morning"; "At a Bar in Charlotte Amalie"; "The Christian Roomates"; "My Lover Has Dirty Fingernails"; "Harv Is Plowing Now"; "The Music School."; "The Rescue"; "The Dark"; "The Bulgarian Poetess"; "The Family Meadow"; "The Hermit."

Bech: A Book. New York: Knopf, 1970. Contents: "Foreward." "Rich in Russia"; "Bech in Rumania"; "The Bulgarian Poetess"; "Bech Takes Pot Luck"; "Bech Panics"; "Bech Swings?"; "Bech Enters Heaven." "Appendix A"; "Appendix B."

Museums and Women and Other Stories. New York: Knopf, 1972. Contents: "Museums and Women"; "The Hillies"; "The Day of the Dying Rabbit"; "The Deacon"; "I Will Not Let Thee Go, Except Thou Bless Me"; "The Corner"; "The Witnesses"; "Solitaire"; "The Orphaned Swimming Pool"; "When Everyone Was Pregnant"; "Man and Daughter in the Cold"; "I Am Dying, Egypt, Dying"; "The Carol Sing"; "Plumbing." "The Sea's Green Sameness"; "The Slump"; "The Pro"; "One of My Generation"; "God Speaks"; "Under the Microscope"; "During the Jurassic"; "The Baluchitherium"; "The Invention of the Horse Collar"; "Jesus on Honshu." "Marching Through Boston"; "The Taste of Metal"; "Your Lover Just Called"; "Eros Rampant"; "Sublimating."

Poetry

The Carpentered Hen and Other Tame Creatures. New York:
    Harper and Brothers, 1958.
Telephone Poles and Other Poems. New York: Knopf, 1963.
Verse. Greenwich, Connecticut: Fawcett, 1965. [Reprints
    The Carpentered Hen and Telephone Poles]
Midpoint and Other Poems. New York: Knopf, 1969.

Children's Books

(Adaptor.) <u>The Magic Flute, by Wolfgang Amadeus Mozart</u>.
New York: Knopf, 1962.

(Adaptor.) <u>The Ring, by Richard Wagner</u>. New York: Knopf,
1964.

<u>A Child's Calendar</u>. New York: Knopf, 1965.

(Adaptor.) <u>Bottom's Dream: Adapted from William Shake-
speare's A Midsummer Night's Dream</u>. New York: Knopf,
1969.

Essays

<u>Assorted Prose</u>. New York: Knopf, 1965. Contents:

"Foreward." "The American Man: What of Him?"; "Anywhere
Is Where You Hang Your Hat"; "What Is A Rhyme?"; "Drinking
From a Cup Made Cinchy"; "On the Sidewalk"; "Why Robert
Frost Should Receive the Nobel Prize"; "Confessions of
a Wild Bore"; "The Unread Book Route"; "Alphonse Peintre";
"Mr. Ex-Resident." "Central Park"; "No Dodo"; "Voices
in the Biltmore"; "Our Own Baedeker"; "Postal Complaints";
"Old and Precious"; "Spatial Remarks"; "Dinosaur Egg";
"Upright Carpentry"; "Crush vs. Whip"; "Metro Gate";
"Cancelled"; "Morality Play"; "Obsfuscating Coverage";
"Bryant Park"; "John Marquand"; "Two Heroes"; "Doomsday,
Mass."; "Grandma Moses"; "Spring Rain"; "Eisenhower's
Eloquence"; "Mostly Glass"; "Three Documents"; "Free
Bee-hours"; "Beer Can"; "Modern Art"; "The Assassination";
"T.S. Eliot." "Hub Fans Bid Kid Adieu." "The Dogwood Tree:
A Boyhood"; "The Lucid Eye in Silver Town"; "My Uncle's
Death"; "Outing: A Family Anecdote"; "Mea Culpa: A Travel
Note"; "Eclipse." "Poetry From the Downtroddendom"; "Snow
from a Dead Sky"; "Franny and Zooey"; "Credos and Curios";
"Beerbohm and Others"; "Rhyming Max"; "No Use Talking";
"Stuffed Fox"; "Honest Horn"; "Faith in Search of Under-
standing"; "Tillich"; "More Love in the Western World";
"A Foreward for Young Readers"; "Creatures of the Air";
"Between a Wedding and a Funeral"; "How How It Is Was";
"Grandmaster Nabokov."

A. PRIMARY SOURCES

    2. Poetry: Uncollected

"Solid Comfort." New Yorker, 31 (18 February 1956), 93.

"Scansion from Exalted Heights." New Yorker, 32 (9

    February 1957), 28-9.

"Reflection." New Yorker, 33 (30 November 1957), 216.

"Simple Life." New Yorker, 33 (18 January 1958), 108.

"Blked." New Yorker, 34 (21 June 1958), 90.

"It Might Be Verse." Reflections, (1959), 10. Source:

    Taylor bibliography, p. 13.

"Yonder Peasant." Contact, 4 (February, 1960), 52.
"Martini." Contact, 4 (February, 1960), 52.
"Parable." Contact, 4 (February, 1960), 53. Source for

    Contact entries: Taylor, p. 14.

"Vision." New Yorker, 36 (7 January 1961), 77.

"Handkerchiefs of Khaiber Khan." New Yorker, 37

    (25 November 1961), 172.

Translation, "The Lament of Abrashka Tertz." New Leader,

    49 (17 January 1966), 3.

"Elm." Polemic, 11 (Winter, 1966), 31. Source: Taylor, p. 18.

Trans., E.A.Evtushenko. "Restaurant for Two." Life, 62

    (17 February 1967), 33.

Trans., E.A. Evtushenko. "Ballad About Nuggets." <u>Life</u>,
62 (17 February 1967), 38.

"Memories of Anguilla, 1960." <u>New Republic</u>, 157
(11 November 1967), 21.

Trans. with Albert C. Todd, Y. Yevtushenko. "America and
I Sat Down Together." <u>Holiday</u>, 44 (November,
1968), 38-42.

"Skyey Developments." <u>New Republic</u>, 160 (8 March 1969, 28.

Trans., Jorge Luis Borges. "The Labyrinth." <u>Atlantic</u>, 223
(April, 1969), 72.

"A l'Ecole Berlitz." <u>New Republic</u>, 161 (6 September 1969),
33.

"Business Acquaintances." <u>New Republic</u>, 161 (4 October
1969), 28.

"South of the Alps." <u>Commonweal</u>, 91 (17 October 1969), 72.

"Upon Shaving Off One's Beard." <u>New Yorker</u>, 46 (16 May
1970), 37.

"On An Island." <u>Saturday Review</u>, 53 (7 November 1970), 29.

"Sunday Rain." <u>Saturday Review</u>, 54 (17 April 1971), 59.

"Marching Through A Novel." <u>Saturday Review</u>, 54 (3 July
1971), 24.

"Wind." <u>Commonweal</u>, 95 (21 January 1972), 373; 99 (16
November 1973), 175.

"Young Matrons Dancing." <u>Saturday Review</u>, 55 (29 January
1972), 6.

"Sand Dollar." <u>Atlantic</u>, 229 (March, 1972), 43.

"A Bicycle Chain." <u>New Yorker</u>, 48 (15 April 1972), 48.

"Sunday." <u>The American Scholar</u>, 41 (Summer, 1972), 389.

"Insomnia the Gem of the Ocean." <u>New Yorker</u>, 48 (16 September 1972), 40.

"To a Waterbed." <u>Harper's</u>, 245 (December, 1972), 66.

"The Cars in Caracas." <u>New Yorker</u>, 48 (30 December 1972), 27.

"Phenomena." <u>New Yorker</u>, 49 (24 February 1973), 38.

"Phi Beta Kappa Poem, Harvard, 1973." Cambridge, Mass.: Harvard University News Office release, 12 June 1973, [1]-7.

"Rubble of Ruined Temples." <u>Beverly</u> (Mass.) <u>Times</u>, 12 January 1970. Source: Ipswich Public Library files.

A. PRIMARY SOURCES

   3. Periodicals: Uncollected Short Stories

"Vergil Moss." New Yorker, 35 (11 April 1959), 99-105.

"Archangel." Big Table, II, 5 (1960), 78-79. Source:
    Taylor bibliography, p. 22.

"Unstuck." New Yorker, 37 (3 February 1962), 24-27.

"Homage to Paul Klee: or, A Game of Botticelli."
    The Liberal Context, No. 12 (Fall, 1964), 8-12.

"The Wait." New Yorker, 43 (17 February 1968), 34-96.

"Love: First Lessons." New Yorker, 47 (6 November 1971),
    46-47.

"Tarbox Police." Esquire, 77 (March, 1972), 85-86.

"Commercial." New Yorker, 48 (10 June 1972), 30-32.

"Believers." Harper's, 245 (July, 1972), 86-87.

"How to Love America and Leave It at the Same Time."
    New Yorker, 48 (19 August 1972), 25-27.

"The Gun Shop." New Yorker, 48 (25 November 1972), 42-47.

"Ride." New Yorker, 48 (2 December 1972), 51.

"Son." <u>New Yorker</u>, 49 (21 April 1973), 33-35.

"Daughter, Last Glimpses Of." <u>New Yorker</u>, 49 (5 November 1973), 50-53.

"Nevada." <u>Playboy</u>, 21 (January, 1974), 167-68, 240-42.

"Ethiopia." <u>New Yorker</u>, 49 (14 January 1974), 28-32.

A. PRIMARY SOURCES

    4. Periodicals: Uncollected Reviews, Review Essays

"Nightmares and Daymares." <u>New York Times Book Review</u>, 3 January 1960, pp. 4, 22.

"Books, Briefly Noted." <u>New Yorker</u>, 39 (1 February 1964), 96-100. Portions reprinted in <u>Assorted Prose</u>.

"Death's Heads." <u>New Yorker</u>, 41 (2 October 1965), 216-28.

"The Author As Librarian." <u>New Yorker</u>, 41 (30 October 1965), 223-46.

"The Fork." <u>New Yorker</u>, 42 (26 February 1966), 115-36. Reprinted in Thomas Altizer, ed. <u>Toward a New Christianity: Readings in the Death of God Theology</u>. New York: Harcourt, Brace, and World, 1967, pp. 59-71.

"The Mastery of Miss Warner." New Republic, 154 (5 March
1966), 23-25. Correction in New Republic, 154
(26 March 1966), 40.

"Two Points On a Descending Curve." New Yorker, 42 (7 January
1967), 91-94.

"Nabokov's Look Back: A National Loss." Life, 62 (13
January 1967), 9, 15.

"Behold Gombrowicz." New Yorker, 43 (23 September 1967),
169-76.

"Grove Is My Press, and Avant My Garde." New Yorker, 43
(4 November 1967), 223-38.

"My Mind Was Without a Shadow." New Yorker 43 (2 December
1967), 223-32.

"Questions Concerning Giacomo." New Yorker, 44 (6 April
1968), 167-74.

"Indifference." New Yorker, 44 (2 November 1968), 197-201.

"Albertine Disparue." New Yorker, 45 (15 March 1969),
174-80.

"Love As A Standoff." New Yorker, 45 (28 June 1969), 90-95.

"Van Loves Ada; Ada Loves Van." New Yorker, 45 (2 August
1969), 67-75.

"The View From the Dental Chair." New Yorker 46 (25 April
1970), 133-36.

"Papa's Sad Testament." New Statesman, 80 (16 October
    1970), 489.

"Satire Without Serifs." New Yorker, 48 (13 May 1972),
    135-44.

"Is There Life After Golf?" New Yorker, 48 (29 July 1972),
    76-78.

"From Dyna Domes to Turkey Pressing." New Yorker, 48
    (9 September 1972), 115-24.

"In Praise of the Blind, Black God." New Yorker, 48
    (21 October 1972), 157-67.

"The Translucing of Hugh Person." New Yorker, 48 (18
    November 1972), 242-45.

"Polina and Aleksei and Anna and Losnitsky." New Yorker,
    49 (14 April 1973), 145-54.

"Ayrton Fecit." New Yorker, 49 (5 May 1973), 147-49.

"A Sere Life; or, Sprigge's Ivy." New Yorker, 49 (2 June
    1973), 119-22.

"Milton Adapts Genius; Collier Adapts Milton." New Yorker,
    49 (20 August 1973), 84-89.

"Snail on the Stump." New Yorker, 49 (15 October 1973),
    182-85.

"Coffee Table Books for High Coffee Tables." New York Times
    Book Review, 28 October 1973, pp. 4-6.

"Jong Love." New Yorker, 49 (17 December 1973), 149-53.

"Shades of Black." New Yorker, 49 (21 January 1974), 84-94.

"Mortal Games." New Yorker, 50 (35 February 1974), 122-26.

"Inward and Upward." New Yorker, 50 (25 March 1974), 133-40.

"A Messed-Up Life." New Yorker, 50 (8 April 1974), 137-40.

"Sons of Slaves." New Yorker, 50 (6 May 1974), 138-42.

A. PRIMARY SOURCES

    5. Periodicals: Uncollected Articles, Essays

"Notes." New Yorker, 32 (26 January 1957), 28-29.

"And Whose Little Generation Are You? Or, Astrology
    Refined." New Yorker, 33 (5 October 1957), 38-39.

"Comment." Times Literary Supplement, 4 June 1964, p. 473.

"An Arion Questionnaire." Arion, 3 (Winter, 1964), 88-89.

"Letter From Anguilla." (also illustration by John Updike)
    New Yorker, 44 (22 June 1968), 70-80.

"Writers I Have Met." New York Times Book Review, 11
    August 1968, pp. 2, 23.

"Amor Vincit Omnia Ad Nauseam (After Awaking From 'Bruno's
    Dream' by Iris Murdoch, and Falling Into the Nursery)."
    New Yorker, 45 (5 April 1969), 33.

"Precise Language [Reply to Mr. Burgess]." Commonweal,
    84 (22 April 1966), 160-61.

"Introduction." In Pens & Needles: Literary Caricatures
    by David Levine. Boston: Gambit, Inc., 1969, pp. [v]-viii.

"An American in London." The Listener, 23 January 1969, pp. 97-99.

"Views." The Listener, 12 June 1969, pp. 817-18.

John Updike et al. "The Professional Viewpoint." Twentieth Century Studies, 1 (November, 1969), 128.

John Updike et al. "Tributes." Triquarterly, No. 17 (Winter, 1970), 342-43.

"First Lunar Invitational." New Yorker, 48 (27 February 1971), 35-36.

"Henry Bech Redux." New York Times Book Review, 14 November 1971, p. 3.

"Søren Kierkegaard." 'Atlantic' Brief Lives: A Biographical Companion to the Arts. Louis Kronenberger, ed. Boston: Little, Brown and Company, 1971, pp. 428-31.

[John Updike and Walter Iooss, jr.] "The Dawn of the Possible Dream." Sports Illustrated, 36 (21 February 1972), 38-45. (Includes photographs, quotations from Rabbit, Run.)

"Remembrance of Things Past." Horizon, 14 (Autumn, 1972), 102-105.

"The Dilemma of Ipswich." Ford Times, 65 (September 1972), 8-15.

"Golf." New York Times Book Review, 10 June 1973, pp. 3, 20.

"Foreward." In Soundings in Satanism. Francis J. Sheed, ed. New York: Sheed and Ward, 1973, pp. vii-xii.

"Foreward." In <u>The Harvard Lampoon Centennial Celebration,</u>
   <u>1876-1973</u>. Martin Kaplan, ed. Boston: Atlantic Monthly
   Press, 1973, pp. [v,vi,] 260-64.
"Confessions of a Committee Chairman." <u>Boston Review of the</u>
   <u>Arts</u>, 2, No. 5. Source: Ipswich Public Library files.

A. PRIMARY SOURCES
   6. Interviews

Gado, Frank, ed. "A Conversation with John Updike." <u>The Idol</u>
   (Union College, NY), 47 (Spring, 1971), 3-32. Reprinted
   in his <u>First Person: Conversations on Writers and</u>
   <u>Writing</u>. Schenectady: Union College Press, 1973, pp.
   80-109. Collection of interviews with Wescott, Dos
   Passos, Warren. Barth, Coover, and Updike.

McCullough, David. "Eye on Books." <u>Book of the Month Club</u>
   <u>News</u>, July 1974, pp. 6-7. Brief interview with Updike
   after publication of <u>Buchanan Dying</u>.

Nichols, Lewis. "Talk with John Updike." <u>New York Times</u>
   <u>Book Review</u>, 7 April 1968, pp. 34-35. An interview
   conducted with Updike after the publication of <u>Couples</u>.
   In it, he speaks of writing a piece about President
   Buchanan and "recourt[ing] the muse of poetry. . . ."

Raymont, Henry. "John Updike Completes a Sequel to
Rabbit, Run." New York Times, 27 July 1971, p. 22.
Interview conducted shortly before the publication of Rabbit Redux. Updike comments on his
new novel and his work: "Once I had lots of theories
about how to write; I've forgotten most of
them."

Rhode, Eric. "Grabbing Dilemmas: John Updike Talks About
God, Love, and the American Identity." Vogue, 157
(February, 1971), 140-41, 180-85. Reprints most
of the Listener interview published in 1969.

_____. "John Updike Talks to Eric Rhode About the
Shapes and Subjects of His Fiction." The Listener,
19 June 1969, pp. 862-64. BBC interview in which
Updike discusses several of his novels, his
feelings about issues (religion, ministers, sex,
marriage), and his future plans. It was conducted
between the publication of Couples and Midpoint.

Rubins, Josh. "Industrious Drifter in Room 2." Harvard
Magazine, 76 (May, 1974), 42-45, 51. Interesting
interview conducted after Buchanan Dying, in which
Updike discusses work habits and his novels.

Samuels, Charles Thomas. "The Art of Fiction XLIII: John
Updike." <u>Paris Review</u>, 45 (Winter, 1968), 84-117.
The first published interview with Updike, conducted
just after the publication of <u>Couples</u>. After speaking
to Samuels, he insisted upon revising and editing the
answers. "The result is a fabricated interview--in
its modest way, a work of art."

"Updike Lauds National Medalist E.B. White." <u>Wilson Library</u>
<u>Bulletin</u>, 46 (February, 1972), 489-90. This news item
reprints excerpts from Updike's speech in Lincoln
Center Library at the ceremony to honor E.B. White
with the National Medal for Literature. The text of
White's acceptance speech is also included.

A. PRIMARY SOURCES

   7. Records, Tapes, Miscellaneous

"Development of the American Short Story: The Short Story
Today." Pleasantville, NY: Educational Audio Visual,
Inc. Record.

"How to Read and Understand Short Fiction." Pleasantville,
NY: EAV, Inc., 1971. Filmstrip.

"John Updike Reads John Updike." New York: CMS Records,
Inc. Selections from "Lifeguard" and <u>The Centaur</u>.

"Modern American Literature: Into the 1970s." New York:
    EAV, Inc. Record.

"Selections from Bech: A Book." Boston: Fassett Recording
    Studio, 14 July 1970. Record in Woodbury Poetry Room,
    Lamont Library, Harvard.

"Selections from his Work Read by the Author." With intro-
    duction by Walter Kaiser. Cambridge, Mass.: "Morris
    Gray Lecture," 23 April 1964. Tape in Woodbury Room.

"Spoken Arts Treasuries of 100 Modern American Poets
    Reading Their Poems." Vol. 18 New Rochelle, NY:
    Spoken Arts, Inc. Record.

"The Poet at Work." Tape with Herb Kenny. Boston: WGBA
    Radio station, 8, 9 May 1971. In Woodbury Room.

"U.S.A. Writers." Educational Television Network. Updike
    television interview, noted in Bryant Wyatt (p. 42).

A. PRIMARY SOURCES

   8. Limited and Rare Editions and Reprints

Dog's Death. Cambridge, MA: Lowell House, 1965. Poem
    reprinted in Midpoint. Broadside sheet limited
    edition of 100. Copy in Houghton Library, Harvard.

Erratum copy, The Music School. New York: Knopf, 1966.
    First edition has lines of poetry transposed in
    "The Madman," p. 46. Copy in Patterson Room, University
    of Louisville.

The Angels. Pensacola, FL: King and Queen Press, 1968.
    New Yorker poem reprinted in Midpoint. Published in
    limited edition of 150. Copy in Library of Congress.

Three Texts from Early Ipswich. Ipswich, MA: Seventeenth
    Century Day Committee of the Town of Ipswich, 1968.
    Selected readings from historical texts in narrative
    form. Personal copy.

Bath After Sailing. Monroe, Connecticut: Pendulum Press, 1968.
    Poem published in limited edition of 125 copies. Copies
    in Patterson Room of University of Louisville and
    Woodbury Room, Lamont Library, Harvard.

The Dance of the Solids. New York: Scientific American,
    1969. Poem reprinted in Christmas-card format from
    Scientific American and Midpoint. Copy in slipcase
    in Library of Congress.

The Indian. Blue Cloud Quarterly, 17 (1971?), 2-7. Essay
    reprinted in pamphlet form. Originally published in
    New Yorker and The Music School. Personal copy and
    Houghton, Harvard.

Warm Wine, An Idyll. New York: Albondocani Press, 1973.
    Short story printed in limited edition of 150. Copy
    in Thurber Room, Ohio State University.

Six Poems. New York: Aloe Editions, n.d. Source: Letter
    from Updike.

A Good Place. New York: Aloe Editions, 1973. Essay reprinted
    from Ford Times. Limited edition of 26 copies, two
    of which are in the Ipswich Public Library and the
    Ipswich Historical Society (Whipple House).

On Meeting Authors. Newburyport, MA: Wickford Press, 1968.
    Essay reprinted from New York Times. Limited edition
    of 250. Copies in Library of Congress and Houghton.

B. SECONDARY SOURCES

1. Books, Chapters in Books, Dissertations

Aldridge, John W. "An Askew Halo for John Updike."
Saturday Review, 53 (27 June 1970), 25-27, 35.
Reprinted as "John Updike and the Higher Theology"
in his The Devil in the Fire: Retrospective Essays
on American Literature and Culture, 1951-1971. New York:
Harper's Magazine Press, 1972, pp. 195-201. This
essay reviews Bech: A Book and the Hamilton's
Elements (see p. 23). While the bulk of his essay
assails the overwriting of Elements, Aldridge sees
Bech as a shift in Updike's style: "perhaps briefly
but one hopes for good, Updike has overcome his
addiction to obliqueness and stylistic preciosity
and written as straightforwardly and compellingly as
he has ever written."

Burchard, Rachael C. John Updike: Yea Sayings. Carbondale:
Southern Illinois University Press, 1971. Although
she believes that "Updike reaches his highest range
of accomplishment" in his short fiction, Burchard
devotes less than 30 of 159 pages to the short
stories of Updike. She begins her study with a

consideration of Updike's poetry and then explains briefly each novel.

Carlson, Constance Hedin. "Heroines in Certain American Novels." Dissertation Abstracts International, 32 (1972), 5175A (Brown). Updike's heroines are explored because Updike is "a novelist whose medium is the interaction of the male and female characters." Carlson also examines Wharton and Scott Fitzgerald.

Detweiler, Robert. John Updike. New York: Twayne, 1972. Explicates Updike's works and places them in a general framework based upon Updike's themes. It includes a short bibliography and deals with Updike's books through Redux.

Falke, Wayne C. "The Novel of Disentanglement: A Thematic Study of Lewis's Babbitt, Bromfield's Mr. Smith and Updike's Rabbit, Run." Dissertation Abstracts, 28 (1967), 194A (Michigan). Examines ways in which fictional characters attempt to disentangle themselves

from "nets," and "find freedom through a personal
rebellion." Falke also examines criticism of
these novels.

Flint, Joyce M. "In Search of Meaning: Bernard Malamud,
Norman Mailer, John Updike." Dissertation Abstracts
International, 30 (1969), 3006A (Washington State).
"Updike concludes that relativism and the populari-
zation of the liberal-humanitarian dream have
literally changed the consciousness of Americans."
She notes Updike's stress on faith; without faith,
"man cannot satisfy his deepest need: a belief in
immortality."

Galloway, David D. "The Absurd Man as Saint." In his
The Absurd Hero in American Fiction: Updike, Styron,
Bellow, Salinger. Rev. ed. Austin: University of Texas
Press, 1970, pp. 21-50, 184-208. One of the first
books published which dealt with Updike at any length
(and was the first dissertation on Updike). It contains
the first checklist of his works and presents him as
an existentialist writer. The revised edition is
prefaced by a discussion of Couples.

Gasca, Eduardo. Literatura de la Tierra Baldia: John
    Updike. Caracas: Universidad Central de Venezuela,
    1969. This short (106 pages) book places Updike
    in a tradition descendant from T.S. Eliot and
    Jung: "the usual example of the histories of the waste
    land are characterized by the presence of essential,
    constant elements: The silence of God...The arrival of
    the hero-seeker...The idea of death and resurrection...
    the archetypes of the christian."

Gass, William H. "Cock-a-doodle-doo." New York Review of
    Books, 11 April 1968, p. 3. Reprinted in his Fiction
    and the Figures of Life. New York: Knopf, 1970, pp.
    206-11. Gass allows that "Many passages, countless
    details, are nothing less than acts of genius."
    Nevertheless, Couples fails in several aspects:
    "The symbolism is sometimes oppressive"; "the
    religious parallels aren't convincingly drawn"; and
    "The interior monologues seem badly imitated Joyce."
    The novel, like the weathervane, "still looks like
    a cold colonial cock to me."

Gilman, Richard. "The Youth of an Author." New Republic,
148 (13 April 1963), 25-27. Reprinted as "Fiction:
John Updike" in his The Confusion of Realms. New
York: Random House, 1970, pp. 62-68. This review of
The Centaur pans the novel as "a virtuoso act of
evasion." It is "a sly exercise, a piece of bravado,
an evasion and a deal flat ground from which, we
may hope, its extraordinarily endowed author can
only rise."

Hamilton, Alice and Kenneth. John Updike: A Critical
Essay. Grand Rapids: William B. Eerdmans, 1967.
This 48-page pamphlet attempts to create an overview of Updike's works through The Music School
(1966). The Hamiltons provide a short sketch of each
book and place it in a thematic (religious)
structure. A short bibliography is appended.

_____. The Elements of John Updike. Grand Rapids:
Eerdmans, 1970. Elements was the first full-length
bool on Updike. Although it suffers from overwriting

(see Aldridge, p. 19), the book is valuable
since it contains thorough discussions of each of
Updike's works. The authors attempted "simply to lay
down some guide lines that might help readers to
approach Updike's work with some degree of sympathetic
understanding."

Hamilton, Alice. "Between Innocence and Experience:
From Joyce to Updike." Dalhousie Review, 49 (Spring,
1969), 102-109. Revised and reprinted in Elements,
pp. 13-26. Professor Hamilton compares Updike's
"You'll Never Know, Dear, How Much I Love You"
(Pigeon Feathers) and Joyce's "Araby." Both stories
relate the initiation experience of a young boy at
a fair.

Harper, Howard M. Jr. "John Updike: The Intrinsic
Problems of Human Existence." In his Desperate Faith:
A Study of Bellow, Salinger, Mailer, Baldwin and
Updike. Chapel Hill: University of North Carolina
Press, 1967, pp. 162-90. Harper postulates that Updike's
characters "see a universe endowed with a rich human
meaning, and they feel a tragic sense of loss at the
erosion of that meaning by time and cosmic

indifference." In his fiction, "Updike shows that
man achieves goodness by wanting the freedoms of
others, and by unselfish love." Harper traces this
theme through Updike's early novels and stories
(through Of the Farm).

Hicks, Granville. "John Updike." In his Literary Horizons:
A Quarter Century of American Fiction. New York: New
York University Press, 1970, pp. 107-33. The Updike
section of this collection of essays reprints Hicks'
Saturday Review book reviews of Updike's works: The
Poorhouse Fair, Rabbit, Run, Pigeon Feathers, The
Centaur, Assorted Prose, Of the Farm, The Music School,
Couples. In his "Afterword," he writes, "it is more
sensible to praise [Updike] for what he has done
than to condemn him for not doing what we think he
could and should have done."

_____. "God Has Gone, Sex Is Left." Saturday Review,
51 (6 April 1968), 21-22. Reprinted in his
Literary Horizons. Not only is Piet "not quite real,"
Hicks writes in this review of Couples, but "the book
is not different from what Updike has written before
but simply more--more couples, more coupling, more
trouble."

Hiller, Catherine. "Personality and Persona: The
        Narrators in John Updike's Fiction." Dissertation
        Abstracts International, 33 (1973), 4416A
        (Brown). "As Updike makes his presence felt most
        forcefully through his narrators, it is on these
        that I concentrate: on both the fully realized
        persona who participates in the events he recounts and
        on the implicit narrator 'Updike's' imagined world."
        She examines each of Updike's books of fiction
        in terms of narration.

Kazin, Alfred. "Professional Observers: Cozzens to
        Updike." In his Bright Book of Life: American
        Novelists and Storytellers from Hemingway to Mailer.
        Boston: Little, Brown, and Co., 1973, pp. 95-124.
        Kazin pictures Updike as a peculiarly American
        writer; "Updike is a novelist of society who sees
        society entirely as a fable." Updike's "real
        subject--the dead hand of 'society,' the fixity of
        institutions--has gone hand in hand with the only
        vision of freedom as the individual's recognition
        of God."

Larsen, Richard B. "The Short Stories of John Updike."
    Dissertation Abstracts International, 34 (1973),
    2634A (Emory). Larsen sees Updike's short stories
    in three divisions, "based upon stylistic and
    thematic approaches to fictional material":
    "predominantly epiphanal, ironical, or lyrically
    meditative in mode." He also treats Updike's novels
    as "characteristic patterns of the author's
    thoughts...."

Lodge, David. "Post-Pill Paradise Lost: John Updike's
    Couples." Reprinted in his The Novelist at the
    Crossroads, and Other Essays on Fiction and
    Criticism. Ithaca, NY: Cornell University Press,
    1971, pp. 237-44. Lodge's essay on Couples relates
    the novel to Freud, and Hawthorne's The Blithedale
    Romance. In Couples, "Updike has taken a large abstract
    theme about contemporary culture and embodied
    it in a densely-textured novel about a particular
    social milieu." While this theme works in the
    first half of the novel, the second half's
    dependence upon Piet and Foxy is burdensome; "they
    are not sufficiently realized to sustain it."

Markle, Joyce B. Fighters and Lovers: Theme in the Novels
of John Updike. New York: New York University Press,
1973. Markle lists what she considers Updike's major
themes: "the flight from death; the need for what I
call 'Lovers' (characters who give a feeling of
stature and specialness to others); evidence, such
as handicraft, of man's impact on his world; the
sources of man's sense of importance; man's abilities
and responsibilities in relating to the members of his
society; and so forth." She analyzes Updike's novels
in thematic terms.

Nadon, Robert J. "Urban Values in Recent American Fiction:
a Study of the City in the Fiction of Saul Bellow,
John Updike, Philip Roth, Bernard Malamud, and
Norman Mailer," Dissertation Abstracts International,
30 (1969), 2543A (Minnesota). "Updike in his earlier
works is especially responsive to the positive
values of the small town." Only Bellow and Mailer
are characterized as "city writers."

Nelson, Doris L. "The Contemporary American Family Novel:
A Study in Metaphor." Dissertation Abstracts International, 31 (1970), 2929A (Southern California).

This study details "family" as metaphor: family as
"some aspect of American society" or as "humanity in
general." The Centaur "explores the precarious
position of mankind in the universe, a race of
creatures between heaven and earth, capable of
dignity and courage."

Plourde, Ferdinand J. Jr. "Time Present and Time Past:
Autobiography as a Narrative of Duration."
Dissertation Abstracts International, 30 (1969), 334A-
335A (Minnesota). Attempts to show why the auto-
biographic narrator constitutes a unique though
currently neglected .'point-of-view' in fiction";
as a case in point, "Pigeon Feathers" is shown
to be an "initiation story ."

Pomeroy, Charles W. "Soviet Russian Criticism 1960-1969 of
Seven Twentieth Century American Novelists."
Dissertation Abstracts International, 32 (1972),
449A (Southern California). In the section "Soviet
Criticism of The Centaur" (pp. 124-32, 137, 180),
Pomeroy examines Russian response to Updike's only
work translated into Russian. He collects Soviet
criticism, summarizes its trends, and indexes it.

"The Centaur is viewed largely in terms of the
aesthetic problem of showing how the realistic and
mythological levels form a single whole."

Rupp, Richard H. "John Updike: Style in Search of a
Center." Sewanee Review, 75 (Autumn, 1967), 693-709.
Reprinted in his Celebration in Postwar American
Fiction, 1945-1967 (with a postscript on Couples).
Coral Gables, FL: University of Miami Press, 1970,
pp. 41-57, 209-18. Rupp theorizes that "Updike's
style circles relentlessly on the circumference of
experience, seeking entry into its center. He simply
has no starting point for natural ceremonies." In
contrast to the style of Cheever, Updike's style
is not "founded on social and religious certitudes";
his ceremonies are "solitary and solemn"; "Updike's
style is highly self-conscious"; "Updike's narrator
is more solemn."

Samuels, Charles T. John Updike. Minneapolis: University
of Minnesota Press, 1969. This 46-page essay is
similar to the other UMPAW essays: it provides an
introduction to Updike's works. He discusses each of
Updike's works through Couples; the section on

Of the Farm is particularly good. He includes a
short bibliography.

Sheed, Wilfred. "Play in Tarbox." New York Times Book
Review, 7 April 1968, pp. 1, 30-33. Reprinted in his
The Morning After: Selected Essays and Reviews. New
York: Farrar, Strauss, and Giroux, 1971, pp. 36-42.
In Couples, "Updike's master subject is the relation
of individual to collective decadence." Sheed
explores the roles assigned to Freddy (priest) and
Piet (scapegoat) and shows how these characters
function in the novel. The development of these
characters is juxtaposed with the flatness of the
other characters; Sheed suggests that even if the
flatness is deliberate, Updike pays a "slight cost in
psychological precision."

Sokoloff, B.A. and David E. Arnason. John Updike: A
Comprehensive Bibliography. Darby, PA: Darby Press,
1970; Folcroft, PA: Folcroft Press, 1971; Norwood,
PA: Norwood Press, 1973. This bibliography has a
remarkable printing history and has been printed in
a limited edition (Folcroft). But it is incomplete
and adds nothing substantial to the 1968 Taylor

bibliography. There are no entries after 1969, and it
does not include Updike's 1969 <u>Bottom's Dream</u>.

Strasberg, Mildred P. "Religious Commitment in Recent
American Fiction: Flannery O'Connor, Bernard Malamud,
John Updike." <u>Dissertation Abstracts International</u>,
32 (1972), 6457A (SUNY-Stony Brook). "To accept
one's self and the other, to know the world as
both good and evil, to refuse and hate God no
matter what the excuse, to reject fate and love
destiny--these are the injunctions one notes in these
writers under consideration."

Tanner, Tony. "The American Novelist as Entropologist."
<u>London Magazine</u>, 10 (October, 1970), 5-18. Reprinted
as "Everything Running Down" in his <u>City of Words:</u>
<u>American Fiction, 1950-1970</u>. New York: Harper and
Row, 1971, pp. 141-52. Tanner examines the use of
"entropy" as a theme in American fiction. In passing,
he mentions Updike as one author concerned with
entropy.

_____. "A Compromised Environment." In his <u>City of Words</u>.
Pp. 273-94. "Just how people live with and within
that compromise ⌈of suburbia and middle-class
existence⌋, and how they die of it, is Updike's
avowed subject." Tanner examines entropy in the
fiction of Updike: "Those of his characters who
'run' do so, among other things, from the entropic
facts of life."

Taylor, C. Clarke. <u>John Updike: A Bibliography</u>. Kent, OH:
Kent State University Press, 1968. This Serif Series
bibliography is thorough and generally accurate.
It lists Updike's works from high school and college,
and all collected and uncollected works since 1954.
It annotates much of the criticism and review of his
work. It is complete through July,1967 and supplements
Galloway's 1966 checklist (see p. 21).

Taylor, Chet H. "The Aware Man: Studies in Self-Awareness
in the Contemporary Novel." <u>Dissertation Abstracts
International</u>, 32 (1972), 5246A (Oregon). An essay
on Updike and contemporary writers explaining the
"new awareness of the conscious self in the midst
of an absurd society and universe."

Taylor, Larry E. <u>Pastoral and Anti-Pastoral Patterns in
John Updike's Fiction</u>. Carbondale: Southern Illinois
University Press, 1971. Taylor examines the tradition
of pastoral and anti-pastoral literature from Third
Century, B.G. He then traces this pattern in American
literature from the Puritans to the present, viewing
Updike as the foremost contemporary writer in this
mode. He discusses the novels through <u>Bech: A Book</u> in
these terms, and summarizes Updike's literary career
as being from "pastoral Olinger to anti-pastoral
Manhattan."

Vargo, Edward P. "The Necessity of Myth in Updike's <u>The
Centaur</u>." <u>Publications of the Modern Language Associa-
tion</u>, 88 (May, 1973), 452-60. Reprinted in his
<u>Rainstorms and Fire: Ritual in the Novels of John
Updike</u>. Port Washington, NY: Kennikat Press, 1973,
pp. 81-103. Vargo believes critics who dismiss
Updike's use of mythology in <u>The Centaur</u> misread the
novel. To Vargo, "Not only is the mythic parallel
artful, but it is also necessary to take us beyond
the confines of the immediate, to objectify the
implicit religious institution felt by the characters
throughout the novel." He asserts that the entire
novel is a narration by Peter, in which he comes to
realize the sacrifice his father made for him. Vargo's
book is the most thoughtful work yet written on Updike.

Warner, John M. "Charity in 'A Gift From the City.'" In
    Barbara McKenzie, ed. The Process of Fiction:
    Contemporary Stories and Criticism. New York:
    Harcourt, Brace, Jovanovich, 1974. A promotional
    flyer for Harcourt included mention of this volume.
    Apparently, the article explicates "A Gift From the
    City," from The Same Door.

Wyatt, Bryant N. "Supernaturalism in John Updike's
    Fiction." Dissertation Abstracts International, 31
    (1971), 4802A (Virginia). Wyatt claims that the
    fiction suggests "a desire to come to terms with
    the problem of waning spiritual values in contemporary
    America under the impact of industrial advancement,
    which poses the threat of an enveloping philosophy
    of secular humanism."

(B. SECONDARY SOURCES)

2. Periodical Articles and Reviews

I. General Articles on Updike's Works

Bellman, Samuel. "Two Part Harmony: Domestic Relations
and Social Vision in the Modern Novel." California
English Journal, 3 (1967), 31-41. Source: 1967
MLA Bibliography, # 9714.

Brewer, Joseph E. "The Anti-Hero in Contemporary Literature." Iowa English Yearbook, 12 (1967), 55-60.
Source: AES, 11, February 1968, # 468.

"Devil's Advocate." Time, 102 (23 July 1973), 69.
Reprints portions of Updike's "Foreward" to Francis J.
Sheed, ed. Soundings in Satanism. New York: Sheed
and Ward, 1973, pp. vii-xii; in the essay, Updike
speculates about the possibility of the devil.

Duffy, Martha. "Locked in a Star." Time, 97 (8 March
1971), 80-81. A review of Enchantment, by Linda
Grace Hoyer (Boston: Houghton Mifflin, 1971),
Updike's mother. The novel "obliquely manages to re-
create the emotional blizzard that made ⌈John⌋ into
an artist."

Finkelstein, Sidney. "The Anti-Hero of Updike, Bellow, and
   Malamud." American Dialog, 7 (Spring, 1972), 12-14, 30.
   Finkelstein delivers a harsh message: by depicting
   America as hopelessly repulsive and unhappy, these
   three novelists "not only dwindle as novelists, but
   [also] as men." The heroes of these writers should be
   ordinary men, rather than defeatist anti-heroes, says
   Finkelstein.

Gallagher, Michael P. "Human Values in Modern Literature."
   Studies: An Irish Quarterly Review, 57 (Summer, 1968),
   142-53. Source: AES, 13, March 1970, #2153.

Gallego, Candido Perez. "La Novelistica de John Updike."
   Arbor, 82 (July/August, 1972), 73-84 (355-66).
   Source: 1972 MLA, # 10464.

Gindin, James. "Megalotopia and the WASP Backlash: The
   Fiction of Mailer and Updike." Centennial Review, 15
   (Winter, 1971), 38-52. Focuses primarily on fiction
   as social and religious commentary. He argues that
   Updike's vision is a return to the past, a more simple era.

Graham, K. "Fighting Fiction." The Listener, 1 January 1970,
   p. 24. Review of two books, one of them a Penguin
   anthology (Penguin Modern Stories 2, ed. Judith
   Burnley) which includes "The Wait" and "Man and
   Daughter in the Cold."

Gratton, Margaret. "The Uses of Rhythm in Three Novels
    by John Updike." The University of Portland Review,
    21 (Fall, 1969), 3-12. Source: AES, 14, May 1971,
    # 2887.

Hainsworth, J.D. "John Updike." Hibbert Journal, LXV
    (Spring, 1967), 115-116. Source: Vargo, Rainstorms,
    p. 222.

Hill, John S. "Quest for Belief: Theme in the Novels of
    John Updike." Southern Humanities Review, 3
    (September, 1969), 166-75. Unable to find reference;
    source: MLA, 1969, # 7868 and Vargo, Rainstorms,
    p. 223.

Kazin, Alfred. "Our Middle-Class Storytellers." Atlantic,
    222 (August, 1968), 51-55. In reviewing an anthology,
    Kazin remarks that in New Yorker fiction nothing
    happens. "This is the plight of the middle-class
    imagination: always to feed oneself a spectator,
    a conscience, a memory only . . . ."

Killinger, John. "The Death of God in American Literature."
Southern Humanities Review, II (Spring, 1968), 149-72.
Source: AES, 12, May 1969, # 1697.

Meyer, Arlin G. "The Theology of John Updike." The Cresset,
34 (October, 1971), 23-25. Meyer reviews John Updike:
Yea Sayings, Rachael Burchard; The Elements of
John Updike, Alice and Kenneth Hamilton; and Pastoral
and Anti-Pastoral Patterns in John Updike's Fiction,
Larry Taylor. He notes that Updike's reputation
"rests on his work rather than on his personality."

Peter, John. "The Self-Effacement of the Novelist."
Malahat Review, 8 (October, 1968), 119-128. This
review-essay of Among Thieves by George Cuomo (New
York: Doubleday, 1968) distinguishes between
novelists and lyricists and masculine and feminine
modes of novels; Peter places Updike with feminine
lyricists: "Updike could almost be viewed as the
inevitable fictional product of the literary move-
ment concurrent with his formative years, the New
Criticism. He is, that is to say, a lyricist
born and made."

Petillon, Pierre-Yves. "Le Desespoir de John Updike."
Critique, 25 (November, 1969), 972-77. This essay
reviews the French translations of Rabbit, Run,
The Centaur, Pigeon Feathers, Of the Farm, and
Couples.

Petter, H[enri]. "John Updike's Metaphoric Novels."
English Studies, 50 (April, 1969), 197-206.
Explores the issue of communication in Updike's
novels through Couples and sees this issue in terms of
confrontations with creation, with society, and with
the characters themselves. Updike's themes are "the
individual's consistency, human relations, man's
attempts at grasping the meaning of existence, mind
spirit." Petter concludes that the "created order of
Updike's novels is a metaphor for the order which
his characters come to discover as a need."

Raban, Jonathon. "Exactitudes." New Statesman, 78
(28 November, 1969), 783-4. Reviews the
Penguin Modern Stories, 1 and 2, which contain
several Updike short stories.

"Sprinters and Splinters." <u>Times Literary Supplement</u>, 19
    March 1970, p. 297. Review of the <u>Penguin Modern
    Stories</u>, 2 and 3, which notes the "splendid
    value" of "The Wait."

Suderman, Elmer F. "Art as a Way of Knowing." <u>Discourse</u>,
    12 (Winter, 1969), 3-14. Suderman discusses the
    manner in which poets and writers formulate and
    convey inner feelings. To exemplify lyric short
    stories he uses "Unstuck" <u>New Yorker</u>, 37 (3
    February, 1962), 24-27 . After retelling the simple
    plot he observes that "critics who complain that
    Updike has little to' say often forget that the
    primary function of art, even of the short story, is
    not to make profound observations about the meaning
    of life but to present the forms of feeling for our
    examination."

Waldmeir, Joseph J. "Only an Occasional Rutabaga: American
    Fiction Since 1945." <u>Modern Fiction Studies</u>, 15
    (Winter, 1969/1970), 467-81. "The five trends which
    I identify are the social critical, the accomodationist,
    the beat-absurd-black humorist, the quest, and the
    neo-social critical." This article presents examples

of these trends and authors who fit into its
categories. Updike is seen as a quest writer, one
of the "most significant of the American writers
since 1945, in terms of consistent high caliber
of production and general critical acceptance.... ."

Wyatt, Bryant N. "John Updike: The Psychological Novel in
Search of Structure." Twentieth Century Literature,
13 (July, 1967), 89-96. While Updike is an "experi-
mentalist" novelist, Wyatt believes Updike's "motifs
have not substantially changed--have instead, been
only modilated, varied in emphasis." Three major
themes are time (including death), the family,
and his major concern--self-identity. Wyatt traces
these themes through The Poorhouse Fair, Rabbit, Run,
The Centaur, and Of the Farm; he discusses each novel
in terms of its structure and how theme influences
this structure.

(B. SECONDARY SOURCES)

    2. Periodical Articles and Reviews

       II. Specific Articles on Updike's Works

The Carpentered Hen

Busha, Virginia. "Poetry in the Classroom: 'Ex Basket-
    ball Player.'" English Journal, 59 (May, 1970), 643-5.
    Explicates "Ex Basketball Player" from The
    Carpentered Hen. Busha notes, "It is a tragic realiza-
    tion that Flick has been cut off in the prime of his
    life." She suggests that the poem can be easily
    taught to students.

The Same Door

Friedman, Ruben. "An Interpretation of John Updike's
    'Tomorrow and Tomorrow and So Forth.'" English
    Journal, 61 (November, 1972), 1159-62. Friedman
    explicates Updike's Same Door story "Tomorrow and
    Tomorrow and So Forth" in terms of the fraudulent
    behavior with which it deals. By the examples of
    deceit in the classroom, Updike seems to be saying,
    "life is a fraud, and by extension, so are the class-
    room and its occupants."

Rabbit, Run

Alley, Alvin P. and Hugh Agee. "Existential Heroes: Frank
    Alpine and Rabbit Angstrom." Ball State University
    Forum, 9 (Winter, 1968), 3-5. Compares the existential
    situations of the heroes in Rabbit, Run and Malamud's
    The Assistant. Both search for their "authentic selves
    in a world of irrationality." Finally, Rabbit's running
    becomes "the ultimate assertion of self."

Burhans, Clinton S. Jr. "Things Falling Apart: Structure
    and Theme in Rabbit, Run." Studies in the Novel, 5
    (Fall, 1973), 336-51. The novel is seen in terms of
    its tightening circles which force Rabbit to act as
    he does: "thematically, Updike explores the conditions,
    the relationships between Rabbit and his milieu, which
    explain [the relentless circles]."

Rotundo, Barbara. "Rabbit, Run and A Tale of Peter Rabbit."
    Notes on Contemporary Literature, 1 (May, 1971), 2-3.
    Short note which traces the influence of the fairy
    tale upon the novel.

Standley, Fred L. "Rabbit, Run: An Image of Life." Midwest
    Quarterly, 8 (Summer, 1967), 371-86. A thorough
    explication of the novel in terms of its portrayal of
    "human beings in crisis situations that call for moral
    choices and religious decisions concerning matters of
    life and death."

Stubbs, John C. "The Search for Perfection in Rabbit, Run."
    Critique: Studies in Modern Fiction, 10 (Spring/
    Summer, 1968), 94-101. Pictures Rabbit "as a
    quester for the feeling of immortality." The images
    of circles correspond to the search for perfection
    Rabbit conducts. In the novel, "Updike's purpose is
    to show the dilemma of the man who faces the funda-
    mental human anxiety and tries to combat it."

Suderman, Elmer F. "The Right Way and the Good Way in
    Rabbit, Run." University Review [University of
    Missouri at Kansas City], 36 (October, 1969), 13-21.
    Suderman delineates the character of Rabbit in
    Rabbit, Run and proclaims him to be "an enigmatic
    character." Critics who place judgements on his actions
    are incorrect because his "character cannot be that
    easily impugned, nor can his problem be dismissed
    as a simple choice between right and wrong."
    Suderman points out that in society the good and the
    right are often in conflict and "it is difficult and
    perhaps futile to try to find either."

Pigeon Feathers

Edwards, A.S.G. "Updike's 'A Sense of Shelter.'" Studies
in Short Fiction, 8 (Summer, 1971), 467-68. Edwards
rebuts an earlier note on "A Sense of Shelter"
(Pigeon Feathers), that of R.W. Reising ["Updike's
'A Sense of Shelter,'" SSF, 7 (Fall, 1970), 651-52],
in which Reising argues that William escapes from
his sheltered world. Edwards argues textually that
William's actions are "surely a rejection of even
the possibility of experience." William's dreams
to stay in school and someday teach are seen by
Edwards as a rejection of the world outside school.

Overmyer, Janet. "Courtly Love in the A&P." Notes on
Contemporary Literature, 2 (May, 1972), 4-5. "A&P"
(Pigeon Feathers) is a short story which has as its
referent the romance of courtly love. The cashier in
the store resigns from his position for the honor of
his ladies--shoppers--who he thinks are mistreated.
Ironically, the girls never discover his gallantry.

Porter, M. Gilbert. "John Updike's 'A&P': The Establishment and an Emersonian Cashier." English Journal,
61 (November, 1972), 1155-1158. Examines Sammy,

the heroic clerk in "A&P" (<u>Pigeon Feathers</u>), and
the Emersonian concept of nonconformity. Sammy
asserts his individuality and follows his conscience;
this maturation is the main thrust of the story.

Reising, R.W. "Updike's 'A Sense of Shelter.'" <u>Studies in</u>
<u>Short Fiction</u>, 7 (Fall, 1970), 651-2. Reising takes
exception to a critical introduction to "A&P" in an
anthology edited by Arthur Mizener in which the editor
alleges that William in the story escapes <u>into</u> the
high school, safe and warm. Reising argues textually
that William escapes <u>from</u> the school's safety.

Sykes, Robert H. "A Commentary on Updike's Astronomer."
<u>Studies in Short Fiction</u>, 8 (Fall, 1971), 575-79.
Sykes seems to address himself to those who would
say Updike "bestows this wealth of rhetorical apparatus
on an apparently trivial incident." The plot of
"The Astronomer," from <u>Pigeon Feathers</u>, is simple
yet subtle: the "idol had feet of clay." The innocuous
story hinges on a reversal of roles (the astronomer-
intellectual) and a Heraclitian metaphor.

The Centaur

Alley, Alvin. "The Centaur: Transcendental Imagination and
Metaphoric Death." English Journal, 56 (October, 1967),
982-5. Alley examines the structure and patterns of
The Centaur; "Reading The Centaur is like moving
among dreams." He notes that Updike drew Peter as
having a "transcendental imagination" and "creative
mind." To understand the novel the reader must view
it as being narrated by the young Peter and adult
Peter. It is important to see George Caldwell's death
at the end of the novel as metaphoric, rather than
literal, death.

Knoke, Paul D. "The Allegorical Mode in the Contemporary
Novel of Romance." Dissertation Abstracts International, 32 (1972), 2695A (Ohio University).
"Allegory is a narrative mode in which the author
conspicuously shapes theme and structure by
portraying character and depicting even in the
perspective of an independent frame of reference,
both levels working together in what might be
termed a metaphor of purpose." Knoke examines myth
in The Centaur.

Kort, Wesley A. "The Centaur and the Problem of Vocation."
In his Shriven Selves: Religious Problems in Recent
American Fiction. Philadelphia: Fortress Press, 1972,
pp. 64-89. This chapter in a book concerned with
religious aspects of fiction considers Updike's
topic of occupations: "Work suggests [a person's]
position in life, all of his offices...when conflict
arises between what a person is or wants to be and
what he does or is required to do, the conflict is a
significant one." Kort traces this conflict through
Updike's works, particularly The Centaur.

Myers, David. "The Questing Fear: Christian Allegory in
John Updike's The Centaur." Twentieth Century Literature, 17 (April, 1971), 73-82. Myers refutes critics
who believe myth is mere trapping in The Centaur:
"It is far rather the tragic allegory of a Christian
soul crying 'de profundis,' struggling for truth and
love in a world which is filled with indifference,
hate and death, and which may be beyond redemption
and without transcendence." The novel includes not
only Greek myth but Greek-Christian identities: George
(Chiron-Christ) and Peter (Prometheus-Satan).

Telephone Poles and Other Poems

Ducharme, Edward R. "Close Reading and Teaching." English
    Journal, 59 (October, 1970), 938-42. This article
    explicates "Shillington," a poem in Telephone Poles;
    Ducharme poses study questions and class discussion
    questions. The explication is offered so that teachers
    might use poetry in the classroom: "The explica-
    tion-teaching strategy combination as evidenced in
    these remarks is one way of engaging prospective and
    even practicing teachers in close reading."

Of The Farm

Lurie, Allison. "Witches and Fairies: Fitzgerald to
    Updike." New York Review of Books, 2 December 1971,
    pp. 6-11. This article traces women characters in
    fairy tales and modern literature: "In the classic
    fairy tale there are four principal roles for women:
    the princess, the poor girl who marries the prince,
    the fairy godmother or wise woman, and the wicked
    stepmother or witch." Lurie analyzes Peggy and Mrs.
    Robinson in Of the Farm.

Verse

Matson, Elizabeth. "A Chinese Paradox, But Not Much
    of One: John Updike in His Poetry." Minnesota Review,
    7 (1967), 157-167. This article's title is deceiving;
    actually, Matson praises Updike's poetry: "it is not
    paradoxical that a man who writes excellent prose
    should write excellent poetry." She divides the
    poetry of The Carpentered Hen and Telephone Poles
    into four categories: word plays, social and literary
    criticism, philosophy, and description.

The Music School

"Keeping it Short." Times Literary Supplement, 24 August
    1967, p. 757. Pessimistic review of The Music School
    "A narcissistic self-consciousness infects
    [Updike's] ambition." And, Updike "is evidently
    not smug, but extremely anxious: in the collection
    he has rarely found a form to match his anxiety
    and his large talent."

Baldeshwiler, Eileen. "The Lyric Short Story: The Sketch
    of a History." Studies in Short Fiction, 6 (Summer,
    1969), 443-453. Traces the development of the lyric
    short story from Turgenev through Eudora Welty and
    Updike. The author uses "Leaves" (The Music School)

to exemplify one representative of the modern
American lyrical short story.

Couples

Archer, William H. "Couples." Best Sellers, 15 April 1968,
    pp. 32-33. Short review.

Broyard, Anatole, "Updike's Twosomes." New Republic,
    4 May 1968, pp. 28-30. Broyard reviews Couples
    and is disappointed: "All too often the sexual act is
    armored in metaphors that, like a condom, insulates
    [the novel's] characters from true feeling." This
    may be because, the critic believes, "perhaps only
    the failure of sex leaves the author something he can
    sublimate into art."

"Community Feeling." Times Literary Supplement, 7 November
    1968, p. 1245. In Couples, the "central situation, of
    Piet and Foxy, falls flatter than any American pan-
    cake" because Piet becomes a symbolic rather than a
    actual "suffering man." This review admits to Updike's
    occasional "superb explosion of talent."

Cayton, Robert F. "Couples." Library Journal, 93 (15 March
1968), 1164. A short review of the novel.

Collier, Peter. "Suburban Surfeit." Progressive, 32 (June,
1968), 48. Collier claims that Updike "seems to
have bitten off more than he can conveniently chew."
The novel is "not a satisfying book" since the pⁱ
people in Tarbox seem bored and bewildered.

"Couples." Booklist, 1 June 1968, p. 1129. Short review.
"Couples." Choice, 5 (July-August, 1968), 628. Short
review.
"Couples." Virginia Quarterly Review, 44 (Summer, 1968),
xcvi. Short review.

Cranston, Maurice. "Selected Books." London Magazine, 8
(February, 19699), 94-96. A short review-essay of
Couples and John Hawkes' The Cannibal. Cranston
notes particularly the use of oral sex in Couples
and compares Updike's approach "to that of a moralist,

one with an interest in sex, like D.H. Lawrence."

Dalton, Elizabeth. "To Have and Have Not." Partisan Review,
36 (Winter, 1969), 134-36. Dalton reviews Couples and
accuses Updike of excessive cleverness": "In Updike's
writing the richness of the language seems an un-
controlled surface proliferation, like the growth
of a creeper, indiscriminate and obscuring." She
feels the style is too facile, so that it leads the
reader to believe "that what can be written with such
ease is not worth writing at all."

Detweiler, Robert. "Updike's Couples: Eros Demythologized."
Twentieth Century Literature, 17 (October, 1971), 235-
46. Detweiler urges that in Couples, a critic "must
explore the many facets of the mystical patterns in
order to see how Updike exhausts them and creates
something new, how he works with myth to demythologize
it and suggest a new reality that is indeed the
latest step of a mythic progression. This analysis
must proceed in three steps: the association of the
fictive characters with the mythic personae, the
establishment of the existential concepts residing in
the fictive-mythic action, and the description of a

just-discernable new ontic vision that the novel
reveals."

Ditsky, John. "Roth, Updike, and the High Expense of
    Spirit." University of Windsor Review, 5 (Fall, 1969),
    111-120. Review-essay of Couples and Portnoy's
    Complaint which treats the two as "a sort of diptych,
    a last pair of panels in the sequence 'Man Loving.'"
    Ditsky likes Couples, but offers criticism as well:
    "One cannot separate the intellectually ludicrous
    from the clumsily awful in this novel, and that is
    its enduring weakness." In Part III of his critique
    (the essay part), Ditsky compares the two novels:
    "Couples and Portnoy's Complaint lead us to the same
    point: the realization, in national terms, of the
    significance of the sexual hangup...."

Flint, Joyce. "John Updike and Couples: The WASP'S Dilemma."
    Research Studies, 36 (December, 1968), 340-47. Flint
    examines two criticisms of Updike's work: his subject
    matter, often criticized as trivial, and his alleged
    limited vision. She contends, "It is possible that
    Updike's choice of 'middles' is at least partially
    responsible for the criticism that he lacks 'vision.'"

She feels that Updike's fiction is misunderstood because of "attempts to sidestep Updike's vision"-- that of middles in conflict.

Fremont-Smith, Eliot. "The Evidence in Tarbox." New York Times, 25 March 1968, p. 39. Considers the male characterization in Couples shallow; "Yet Couples does create a universe that in the end quite magically escapes the binds of time and place and point of view, the demands of reality and programed myth."

Fuller, Edmund. "Case For Celibacy." Wall Street Journal, 13 May 1968, p. 16. "Nobody is happy. This is the book's claim to morality." Fuller pans Couples and advises that it is not worth buying: "The language is fashionably coarse, the couplings are described in repetitiously clinical, alternately repellent or ludicrous, detail."

Gordon, David J. "Some Recent Novelists: Styles of Martyr- dom." Yale Review, 58 (Autumn, 1968), 112-126. Gordon reviews seven books, Couples among them. He comments particularly upon Updike's use of "God" in the novel: "Updike himself uses the imaginatively rich word "God"

throughout the book in an annoyingly literal way, as
if he wants to escape not merely psychologism but nat-
uralism, as if he wants doom to be inescapable."

Greenfeld, Josh. "A Romping Set in a Square New England
Town." Commonweal, 88 (26 April 1968), 185-87. To
this reviewer of Couples, Updike proves, "only too
sadly, that you don't have to be a bad writer to come
up with an awful novel; [he proves] that you can be
a good writer and still pull one off, with a little
bit of bad luck." The length of the novel revealed
two faults in the author: "a basically weak sense of
humor and a terrible ear for dialogue." Greenfeld
feels that Updike's career is a "serious and important
and worthwhile literary quest."

Hill, William B. "Couples." America, 118 (4 May 1968),
622. Short review.

Hill, William B. "Fiction." America, 118 (8 Juen 1968),
757. Hill states, "Mr. Updike has written a gamy
but serious book." Although Piet seems to be
struggling for values, "he takes refuge in a
Calvinistic fatalism and evades all efforts of will."

Hope, Francis. "Screwing in Turn." New Statesman, 76
(8 November 1968), 639-40. This review criticizes
the style of Couples; for Hope, the writing is cumber-
some. "At its best, Couples is very good"; he then
qualifies this: "But its best is intolerably clogged
with fine writing." Again, "Couples--stylistically,
not morally--is too much."

Hyman, Stanley Edgar. "Couplings." New Leader, 51 (20 May
1968), 20-21. To this reviewer Couples "is a strong
contender in the most-ill-advised-work-by-a-writer-
of-great-talent-sweepstakes." Hyman notes failings in
the scope, portentousness, symbolism, prose, and
influences. Strengths are noted in Updike's sense of
comedy and use of the incongruous.

Kazin, Alfred. "Updike: Novelist of the New, Post-Pill
America." Washington Post Book World, 7 April 1968,
pp. 1,3. In Couples, Updike scores well as "a
sociologist of all this new American territory,"
and "Above all, Updike knows the overpowering marriage
centeredness of the suburbs...." Kazin accuses Updike
of writing for himself and engaging in "youthful
self-indulgence."

Kermode, F. "Shuttlecock." The Listener, 80 (7 November
     1968), 619. A comparison is drawn between Couples
     and The Good Soldier. Kermode's main objection is
     that "there are too many couples one doesn't care
     about; and even in the big characters, Hanema and
     Thorne the dentist, for example, the muddle or vice
     isn't really in focus."

Kort, Wesley. "Desperate Games." Christian Century, 85
     (23 October 1968), 1340-42. Kort believes Couples
     is "a work preoccupied with the death-and life-
     giving potential in calling, in office."

Maddocks, Melvin. "John Updike's Peyton Place." Life, 64
     (5 April 1968), 8. Deplores the sexual treatment in
     Couples: "Couples is just too busy with coupling
     to relate people for long any other way."

Novak, Michael. "Son of the Group." The Critic, 26 (June-
     July, 1968), 72-74. Review-essay on Couples which
     dwells particularly on Updike's views of the middle

class and religion; Novak notes Updike's "poetic
sense" and "almost absolute control of descriptive
language." Of Couples, Novak concludes, "The discovery
of a new form of paganism is the first order of
business in America."

Price, R.G.G. "New Novels." Punch, 255 (13 November 1968),
710. Short review.

Prichard, William H. "Fiction Chronicle." Hudson Review,
21 (Summer, 1968), 364-76. Review of 10 or
so books (including Couples) and an essay dealing
with the state of American fiction. Pritchard ends
his essay with the observation that Updike seems to
think "Life is very strange and people don't seem
satisfied with what they have. With the exception
of Saul Bellow, no American novelist says this as
strongly as Updike, and adding Mailer to the company
we have our three major novelists. Fiction is still
human."

Smith, Harry. "Bestsellers Nobody Reads." Smith, 10
(November, 1968), 182-184.

Sokolov, Raymond A. "Musical Beds." Newsweek, 71 (8 April
    1968), 125-26. Sokolov comments upon Couples sexual-
    ity: "It requires a feat of rote memory to keep the
    several members of Updike's case separate." He feels,
    though, that Updike "is so good a craftsman that
    he can squeeze much eloquence out of a very marginal
    candidate for our interest."

Tanner, Tony. "Hello, Olleh." Spectator, 221 (8 November
    1968), 658-59. Review-article of Couples which
    compares Updike to Andrew Wyeth and explores Updike's
    view of entropy. Couples is seen as a "serious book,
    then, yet several faults remain." These faults lie
    in Updike's "attempt to establish a real love story
    in the middle of all the random fornications which
    distract Updike's attention."

Thompson, John "Updike's Couples." Commentary, 45 (May,
    1968), 70-73. Thompson compares imagery in Couples
    with imagery in Lolita, and cites passages from both
    novels. He cites problems in reviewing Updike's
    novels ("We cannot tell a story well unless we know

what it means.") Much is made of Updike's concept of
Eros ("Unless I am mistaken, Eros is here done most
grievous dirt").

Trilling, Diana. "Updike's Yankee Traders." Atlantic, 221
(April, 1968), 129-31. Trilling blasts Couples in this
review. While she distinguishes between Updike's
novel and conventional pornography, she notes, "This
much sexual literalness together with this much
verbal debauchery makes a wearying combination, as
wearying as the combination of sexual debauchery and
verbal literalness in conventional pornography." She
pans the style, scope, and "sexual exertions" of
the novel. "The great failure of Mr. Updike's book
is that whatever 'significance' he may have meant to
give it, it has none except such as the reader may
himself supply."

Turner, Michael. "Couples." The Cresset, 31 (September,
1968), 19. "Artistically, there can be little doubt
that Couples is Updike's weakest effort, but I do not
think that it is devoid of content. Updike is just
speaking more pessimistically."

"View From the Catacombs." <u>Time</u>, 91 (26 April 1968),
66-75. The publication of <u>Couples</u> caused this cover
story to be written; it comments upon the novel,
Updike's work, his lifestyle, his working habits.
It contains comments from Updike, pictures of the
author, and a map of fictional Tarbox.

Waller, G.F. "Updike's <u>Couples</u>: A Barthian Parable."
<u>Research Studies</u>, 40 (March, 1973), 10-21. Waller
disagrees with the bulk of <u>Couples</u> criticism: he
argues that the novel "is a major, even prophetic,
novel, which grows out of Updike's fascination with
the spiritual state of historic and contemporary New
England, and is thus consistent with and extends the
dominant interests of Updike's work."

Yglesias, Jose. "Coupling and Uncoupling." <u>Nation</u>, 206
(13 May 1968), 637-38. <u>Couples</u> seems to miss its
point, writes Yglesias. He believes the epigraphs
and jacket cover do not elevate a shallow novel. He
urges Updike to "pay no attention to unappreciative
critics and stick to your interests." He believes a
novel on a grand, involved scale (particularly
<u>Couples</u>) is not Updike's forte.

Midpoint and Other Poems

Adams, Phoebe. "Short Reviews: Books." Atlantic, 223 (June,
1969), 116-18. Short review of Midpoint.

"Answers to Questions Unasked." Times Literary Supplement,
29 January 1970, p. 104. If you found Pound's
Cantos boring, wait until you read Midpoint, this
review says quickly. The typographical collage
pictures "deodorized sex." The poems at the
end are "easily the best."

Brownjohn, Alan. "Dualities." New Statesman, 79 (6 March
1970), 330-32. Review of eleven books of poetry,
including Midpoint. "Updike writes the kind of accomplished comic verse that highly ingenious American
writers seem able to produce almost at will: sardonic,
fashionably frank and self-mocking, and ultimately
pointless."

Demos, John. "Midpoint and Other Poems." Library Journal,
94 (1 April 1969), 1504. Short review.

Fuller, J. "Innocents Abroad." The Listener, 84 (23 July
1970), 122. Brief mention of Midpoint in a review

of seven books of poetry.

Gates, Ann. "John Updike--Wearing His Poet's Hat."
Christian Science Monitor, 15 August 1969, p. 9.
In Midpoint, Gates writes, Updike "exploits
pointillism and its meaning both for the eye and
the I." It is "difficult, intense, and it seems
to me, highly personal."

Hamilton, Alice and Kenneth. "Theme and Technique in
John Updike's Midpoint." Mosaic, 4 (Fall, 1970),
79-106. The Hamiltons explicate thoroughly Updike's
confessional poem, Midpoint. They trace the elements
of Dante, Spenser, Pope, Whitman, and Pound in
Updike's poetry. His "'Midpoint' meditation upon
his life and work shows how he has run counter to
popular values which he believes to be disastrous
both on an individual and on a social level."

Heyen, William. "Sensibilities." Poetry, 115 (March,
1970), 426-29. This essay reviews Midpoint and
three other books of poetry. Updike's work misses
his "own mark." Midpoint's "vision is comic, its
laughter and irony directed at itself."

Bottom's Dream

Heins, Paul. "John Updike, Adapter: Bottom's Dream."
    Horn Book, XLV (December, 1969), 667. Source:
    Vargo, Rainstorms, p. 217.
McConnell, Lynda. "Bottom's Dream." Library Journal,
    95 (15 April 1970), 1643. Short review.

Magid, Nora. "Clear the Stage For a Repeat Performance."
    New York Times Book Review, 9 November 1969, II, pp.
    64-65. Magid pans this adaptation from Midsummer
    Night's Dream: "While most of the text is
    Shakespeare's, the errors put in are unforgivable."
    She notes several distracting deviations from the
    original play, and then notes: "Further, the
    mistakes [even] extend to Warren Chappell's
    illustrations."

Bech: A Book

Algren, Nelson. "Bech: A Book." Critic, 29 (November/
      December, 1970), 84-86. "Bech: A Book is a
      composite cartoon derived from portraits of
      contemporary New York writers." Algren feels that
      the book is not interesting to most readers.

"Bech: A Book by John Updike." New Republic, 163 (11 July
      1970), 27. Short review of Bech.

Bolger, Eugenie. "The New Updike." New Leader, 53 (20 July
      1970), 16-17. Review-essay which claims that in
      addition to "presenting a radically new character,
      Bech: A Book marks the virtual disappearance of
      Updike's distinctive lyric style." Bolger notes
      particularly the techniques of style Updike uses
      in Bech.

Braine, John. "Bourgeois Decadence." Spectator, 24
      October 1970, pp. 480-81. Braine's chief objection
      to Bech: A Book is that "at no point does Bech
      convince one that he is a Jew." He cites several
      incidents which, to Bolger, are examples of un-

realistic Jewish behavior. He also makes general
remarks about contemporary American literature:
"something essential has leaked out of the American
novel."

Broyard, Anatole. "All the Way with Updike." Life, 68
(19 June 1970), 12. "Even as a motherless child,
Bech is one of Updike's best creations." "For the
first time, Updike the esthete has given us a
full-bodied hero, hairy and heavy-set with
humanity."

Coleman, John. "Recognitions." New Statesman, 83 (14
April 1972), 502-503. Short review.

Cowley, Malcolm. "Holding the Fort on Audubon Terrace."
Saturday Review, 54 (3 April 1971), 17, 41-42. In
"Bech Enters Heaven" (Bech: A Book), Bech is
initiated into an honor society. Cowley pinpoints
the society as the National Institute of Arts and
Letters and gives a brief history of the Institute,
the Academy of Arts and Letters, and the American

Academy of Arts and Sciences. Many reviewers have
confused (understandably) the three in reviewing
Bech. Both the Institute and the Academy of Arts
and Letters share the same building on Audubon
Terrace.

Davenport, Guy. "On the Edge of Being." National Review,
22 (25 August 1970), 903-904. Short review.

Donoghue, Denis. "Silken Mechanism." The Listener,
15 October 1970, pp. 524-25. "The théme which
holds these episodes together is the familiar
plaint that people are treated as things."
This reviewer addresses himself particularly to
the organization of Bech: A Book.

Edwards, Thomas R. "Bech: A Book." New York Times Book
Review, 21 June 1970, pp. 1,38. Edwards notes the
resemblance between Bech and his creator. Further,
"Bech: A Book is more than an ethnic stage-turn--
imagining Jewishness imposes a useful discipline
on Updike at this point in his own career, and it
leads to perhaps his best and most attractive book."

Gold, Ivan. "You Really Gets." <u>Nation</u>, 210 (29 June 1970),
791-92. Gold praises Updike's "emotional
exactness" but sees Bech's characterization as
neither Jewish nor artistic: "his artistic anonymity
disqualifies the importance of his art."

Hamilton, Alice and Kenneth. "Metamorphosis Through Art:
John Updike's <u>Bech: A Book</u>." <u>Queen's Quarterly</u>,
77 (Winter, 1970), 624-36. Thorough and critical
review-essay of <u>Bech</u> by the professors who have
written more about Updike than has anyone. They
see "The Bulgarian Poetess" as the central
chapter in the book; the theme of Bech's conflict is
that he is not able to succeed in capturing "his
long-lost mistress, Inspiration." Updike has
pictured Bech as a sexual being who cannot convert
his sexuality into its "poetic equivalent"--art.

Harper, Howard M. Jr. "Trends in Recent Fiction."
<u>Contemporary Literature</u>, 12 (Spring, 1971), 204-
229. In <u>Bech: A Book</u>, the "mild satire is directed,
as it should be, not only at the shallowness and
hypocrisy inherent in the establishment but also at

the vanity and weakness which makes Bech such an easy mark." <u>Bech</u> is one of several novels Harper reviews in this essay.

Kramer, Hilton. "Portrait of the Artist as a Jewish Intellectual." <u>Washington Post Book World</u>, 19 July 1970, p. 3. <u>Bech: A Book</u> is "a literary triumph, and may well be Updike's strongest fictional accomplishment." The novel dramatizes, for Kramer, "the contradictions that separate art as a sacred vocation from the artist as a vulnerable social animal."

Kuehl, Linda. "The Risks in Putting On a Put-On." <u>Christian Science Moniter</u>, 23 July 1970, p. 7. Short review.

Lehmann-Haupt, Christopher. "Updike: A Mensch." <u>New York Times</u>, 11 June 1970, p. 43. Lehmann-Haupt had never been an Updike fan; <u>Bech: A Book</u> changed him: "It succeeds marvelously." The novel has "a touch of lighthearted caricature" that distinguishes it from Updike's earlier works.

"The Lion That Squeaked." Time, 95 (22 June 1970), 82, 84.
The stories in Bech: A Book are seen as "the funniest,
most elegantly written and intelligently sympathetic
renditions available about that happens when a
writer stops being a writer and becomes a culture
object."

Murray, John. "Bech: A Book." Best Sellers, XXX (15 July
1970), 159-60. Source: Vargo, Rainstorms, p. 217.

Murray, Michele. "Profile of a Literary Hustler."
National Catholic Reporter, 24 July 1970, p. 13.
Short review.

Nelson, Barbara. "Bech: A Book." Library Journal, 95
(1 June 1970), 2183. Short review.

"On Not Rocking the Boat." <u>Times Literary Supplement</u>,
   16 October 1970, p. 1183. Bech himself is perhaps too
   shallow, although he is "genuinely loveable." "Bech
   emerges more as the agent of a gleeful revenge
   fantasy than as a wounded hero."

Ozick, Cynthia. "Ethnic Joke." <u>Commentary</u>, 50 (November,
   1970), 106-14. Deals chiefly with Bech's credibility
   as a Jew: "If to be a Jew is to become covenanted,
   then to write of Jews without taking this into account
   is to miss the deepest point of all." Bech, to Ozick,
   is not believable; he "has no reality at all: he is
   a false Jew. . . ."

Perez-Minik, Domingo. "La Novela Extranjera en Espana:
   <u>El Libro de Bech</u>, de John Updike." <u>Insula</u>, 26 (October,
   1971), 6. Source: 1972 <u>MLA</u>, # 10465.

Raban, Jonathon. "Talking Head." <u>New Statesman</u>, 80 (16
   October 1970), 494. Raban points up two aspects of
   <u>Bech</u>: its resemblance to Nabokov's work and its
   autobiographical details. He alludes to its "loveliness
   of style" and decides that it "is a book of desolate
   wit; but Updike never finally manages to reveal
   whose desolation we are witnessing."

Richardson, Jack. "Keeping Up With Updike." New York
Review of Books, 22 October 1970, pp. 46-48.
"Everything about Bech is lean, antic and to the point,
and it has a daring that is supported, rather than
encumbered, by the lessons of tradition." This review-
essay also mentions Couples, The Centaur, and
Rabbit, Run.

Richler, Mordecai. "Porky's Plaint." London Magazine,
10 (November, 1970), 106-108. Richler reviews Bech:
A Book in terms of Updike's "hitherto unsuspected
strain of chutzpah." He gives a general overview
of Updike's place in current American letters
("easily one of the most fluent of contemporary
American writers and also the most engaging") and a
general review of Bech: A Book ("more a string of
loosely-connected stories than a novel [it] is
also episodic and curiously uneven in tone").

S [chickel,] R [ichard]. "Bech: A Book." Harper's, 241
(July, 1970), 102. Brief notice of Bech, which
Schickel believes "is new evidence of [Updike's]

capacity to grow and change and it is, I think,
the most delightful book in his canon."

Sissman, L.E. "John Updike: Midpoint and After." Atlantic,
226 (August, 1970), 102-104. Sissman believes Bech
is "not a major work, but it may be a book of
considerable significance to Updike's development
in the second half of his career." By dividing
Updike's career in halves, Sissman is able to say
that Bech, "at least in part, represents a reprisal,
and a healthy one, against the literary establishment."

S[okolov], R[aymond] A. "Gentile Parody." Newsweek,
75 (15 June 1970), 106. Enthusiastic review of Bech:
A Book: "Still, there is order here, an arc of
despair, of self-hate, that grows from restlessness
to panic."

Townley, Rod. "Bech: A Book." Studies in Short Fiction,
8 (Spring, 1971), 343-4. Townley labels the
book as "the portrait of the artist as a cartoon
of Laocoon, an ironic, fictionally distanced
self-appraisal."

Rabbit Redux

Allen, Bruce D. "Of a Linotype Operator at the Edge of
    Obsolescence." Library Journal, 96 (1 November 1971),
    3640. Short review.

Alter, Robert. "Updike, Malamud, and the Fire This Time."
    Commentary, 54 (October, 1972), 68-74. Alter
    rebuts John Murray Cuddihy's article "Jews, Blacks, and
    the Cold War at the Top" (Worldview, February 1972)
    in which Cuddihy contends that the "Wasp art-novel"
    is in fact "ethnically emasculating" to Jews and
    blacks. The remainder of Alter's article deals with
    Malamud's The Assistant and The Tenants, and with
    Updike's Rabbit Redux. Of Updike's novel Alter states,
    "Rabbit Redux is that rare thing, a convincing
    sequel" because Rabbit "reappears here thoroughly a
    creature of his changed time, caught in its social
    crises, shaped by his class and surroundings as
    they have evolved into the late 1960's."

"Back To Pennsylvania." The Economist, 243 (8 April 1972),
    12. This short review of Rabbit Redux postulates
    that Updike's "main theme is the individual's
    struggle to distinguish his identity from his

environment." Vargo has listed this article as
authored by John Heidenry (Rainstorms p. 218),
but The Economist makes no mention of its author.

[Bannon, Barbara A.] "Rabbit Redux." Publisher's
   Weekly. 202 (18 September 1972), 75. Short precis
   of Rabbit Redux and a notice of promotional
   materials for the novel.

Broyard, Anatole, "Updike Goes All Out At Last." New York
   Times, 5 November 1971, p. 40. Broyard believes this
   is Updike's most accomplished work: "In Rabbit Redux,
   Updike's ear is perfect and he has finally put
   together in his prose all the things that were there
   separately."

Cooke, Michael. "Recent Fiction." Yale Review, 61 (Summer,
   1972), 599-609. This review of eight novels touches
   upon Rabbit Redux and calls it "vintage Updike."
   Cooke recounts some of Updike's "images vibrant"
   and comments upon the ending in which "nothing
   happens."

Davenport, Guy. "Even as the Heather Rage." National Review, 23 (31 December 1971), 1473. Short review.

Gill, Brendan. "A Special Case." New Yorker, 47 (8 January 1972), 83-4. Gill juxtaposes Rabbit Redux with the 1960 Rabbit, Run: "the illuminations of Rabbit Redux cast back upon Rabbit, Run cause it to be seen in a new light, at once brighter and more distressing than the light in which we saw it first." He praises the "immense chances" that Updike took in dealing with Rabbit again, since Run was "complete in itself."

Gill, Brendan. Virginia Quarterly Review, 48 (Spring, 1972), xlviii. Source: Vargo, Rainstorms, p. 218.

Gordon, John. "Updike Redux." Ramparts, 10 (April, 1972), 56-9. Gordon believes that despite weak dialogue in Rabbit Redux, "outside of Bech this is Updike's brightest book, though not his most brilliant."

"The worst parts of Rabbit Redux are when it
threatens to become one of those 'novels of
ideas' like The Shoes of the Fisherman, where the
characters function as debating teams." Gordon
admires Updike, and explains some of his early
hero-worship of the author.

Hamilton, Alice and Kenneth. "John Updike's Prescription
For Survival." Christian Century, 89 (5 July 1972),
740-44. The Hamiltons believe that in Rabbit Redux
"Updike suggests that ours is the confusion of a
world deliberating traveling, like a spacecraft,
toward nothingness." Updike's prescription is to
develop an awareness of time: "Time, rather than
space, is the dimension with human meaning; and
time is not a void, for it is marked by seasons
connecting in definite sequence."

Heidenry, John. "The Best American Novel in a Decade."
Commonweal, 95 (7 January 1972), 332-333. Heidenry
has much applause for Updike in this review of
Rabbit Redux: Updike is "something of a literary
Mr. Jones, whom all other American writers have to

keep up with." "John Updike is not a great
writer but with Norman Mailer and Truman Capote he
is one of only three first-rate prose writers
that this country has." Updike is shown as seeking
for "that 'mysterium americanum'--or whatever it
is--" and Heidenry predicts he will find it.

Hill, William B. "Rabbit Redux." America, 126 (20 May
    1972), 549-60. Short review.

Howes, Victor. "Rerun Rabbit Run." Christian Science
    Monitor, 18 November 1971, p. 11. In a Question-
    Answer mock interview about Rabbit Redux, Howes
    answers that "I'm bothered about what seems to be
    a lack of focus, for want of a better word, on
    Updike's part." Yet he allows, "Some things Updike
    is awfully good at. Descriptions. He has a
    keen sense of the past."

Kennedy, Eileen. "Rabbit Redux." Best Sellers, 31 (15
    December 1971), 429-30. Short review.

Leonard, John. "The Last Work: The Novel, Redux."
New York Times Book Review, 14 November 1971, p. 71.
Leonard surveys the form novels have taken and
concludes that, despite predictions ten years ago to
the contrary, secular news reports--"in other words,
a story about men, women, and children in society"--
are the current novel form: "moral journalism." He
suggests that critics review novels as did Lionel
Trilling: as "literary situations...as cultural
situations...as great elaborate fights about moral
issues...as images of personal being...as having
something to do with literary style."

Lindroth, James R. "Rabbit Redux." America, 126 (29 January
1972), 102-104. Short review.

Locke, Richard. "Rabbit Redux." New York Times Book
Review, 14 November 1971, pp. 1-2, 12-16, 20-24.
Perhaps the best summary of Updike's works and
review of Redux in print, this article surveys Updike's
literary career, works, and Rabbit Redux, and compares
Updike and Mailer. Of Redux, Locke writes that he
"can think of no stronger vindication of the claims

of essentially realistic fiction than this extra-
ordinary synthesis of the disparate elements of contemporary experience."

Lyons, Eugene. "John Updike: The Beginning and the End."
Critique: Studies in Modern Fiction, 14 (Spring/
Summer, 1972), 44-59. This extended review
disparages Updike's novel and all who would praise
it. Lyons writes, "It is a novel so jarring and
offensive to both mind and taste that it is very
likely to send many readers back to its predecessor
Rabbit, Run, published in 1960, to see how they could
have been so wrong." He objects that "none of
the characters is [human]." The most serious
weakness in Rabbit Redux is Updike's "gratuitous
symbol mongering."

Mudrick, Marvin. "Fiction and Truth." Hudson Review, 25
(Spring, 1972), 142-156. Mudrick reviews 16 books,
including Rabbit Redux. John Updike "continues to do
well what he has always done well."

Oldsey, Bernard. "Rabbit Run to Earth." Nation, 214 (10
January 1972), 54, 56. Exalts style and

characterization in the novel and faults
"some force of insight." Oldsey examines the
work and sees Updike as a novelist who works
"mainly with the earthy issues of social and psychological reality."

Prescott, Peter S. "Angstrom's Angst." Newsweek, 78 (15
   November 1971), 124-5. Of Rabbit Redux, Prescott
   asks, "Was the sequel a good idea? Perhaps not,
   though there is much that is the best and simplest
   of Updike in it." He notes "Updike's famous
   obsession with sexual encounters in which no one
   ever seems to have even a passably good time...."

"Rabbit Redux." Choice, 9 (June 1972), 510. Brief notice.

Ricks, Christopher. "Flopsy Bunny." New York Review of
   Books, 16 December 1971, pp. 7-9. Rabbit Redux is
   inconsistent: Updike "vacillates between the
   observantly indiscriminate and the glintingly
   significant, and by the smallest of shufflings
   the apt becomes the pat." It is "likely to do
   retrospective damage to that better book Rabbit, Run."

Samuels, Charles Taylor. "Updike on the Present." New
    Republic, 165 (20 November 1971), 29-30. Samuels
    sees Rabbit Redux in terms of Bellow's Mr. Sammler's
    Planet and assesses Updike's novel as weak in
    "fathoming causes and asserting judgements." The
    final "OK?" of Redux strikes the reviewer as
    inconclusive: "This obscurity makes Updike's final
    refusal to pass judgement particularly disturbing."

Sheppard, R.Z. "Cabbage Moon." Time, 98 (15 November 1971),
    89. Sheppard suspects that in Rabbit Redux "Updike
    also intended a sort of nursery fable for grownups";
    this review offers a brief sketch of the novel and
    remarks that Rabbit's characterization is "far from
    flawless."

Stafford, William T. "'The Curious Greased Grace' of John
    Updike, Some of His Critics, and the American
    Tradition." Journal of Modern Literature, 2 (November,
    1972), 569-575. Stafford reviews Rabbit Redux, its
    reviewers, and Updike's critics (Burchard, Yea
    Sayings; Hamiltons, Elements; and Taylor, Pastoral
    and Anti-Pastoral). Burchard's work "has no
    discernable reasons for existence." Taylor's is

"much more provocative." While the Hamiltons are almost "ideal readers" of Updike, "the over-schematization is often offensive and obtrusive." Stafford reviews <u>Rabbit Redux</u> and responds to Ricks (p. 83) and Locke (p. 81). He seems to belittle criticism, no matter how "crass the comment, however admiring or damning, when set up against the achieved fact of fiction."

Theroux. Paul. "A Has-Been, 10 Years Later." <u>Washington Post Book World</u>, 14 November 1971, pp. 3, 10. "It is a tedious album of the most futile monochromes of Sixties' America; it is leering, erratic, and gimmicky; it is disingenuous and trite. At best it is dull, at worst the shabby outrage of an imagination dulled by indulgence."

Trevor, William. "All Right, Sort Of." <u>New Statesman</u>, 84 (7 April 1972), 462-63. Trevor decries the preoccupation with sex in <u>Rabbit Redux</u> but allows that "what dominates the novel--as it does <u>Rabbit, Run</u> and indeed America itself--is a sense of empti-ness, of death without God, and loneliness in hostile space."

"Unsentimental Education." <u>Times Literary Supplement</u>,

    7 April 1972, p. 385. In this review of <u>Rabbit Redux</u>,

    the critic believes that the reader is treated to

    "seminars," and "Rabbit's conversion is both

    instantly predictable and interminably wordy." The

    book is too obvious and "Updike only rarely manages

    to disguise its obviousness." Although Vargo credits

    Brendan Gill with this review (<u>Rainstorms</u>, p. 218)

    it is unsigned in <u>TLS</u>.

Weber, Brom. "<u>Rabbit Redux</u>." <u>Saturday Review</u>, 54 (27

    November 1971), 54-55. Weber reviews religious points

    made in <u>Redux</u>: "Saint, anti-hero, existentialist man,

    God-seeker, whatever he is, Rabbit marks a dead end

    from which John Updike should make a turnabout."

Museums and Women and Other Stories

Grumbach, Doris. "Suburban Middle Age." New Republic,
    167 (21 October 1972), 30-31. Grumbach notes,
    "Updike's subject matter has now settled into a
    heavy concentration upon suburban middle age." The
    review turns into an essay on form and content with
    regard to Updike's style; she feels we are left "not
    a whit closer than the scholars to the answer."

Hartman, Matthew. "Museums and Women and Other Stories."
    Library Journal, 97 (August 1972), 2649. Short
    review.

Kanon, Joseph. "Satire and Sensibility." Saturday Review
    55 (30 September 1972), 73, 78. With the exception
    of "Other Modes," "the stories in this collection are
    the work of perhaps the finest literary craftsman
    working in America today."

Meyer, Arlin G. "Form, Fluidity, and Flexibility in Recent
    American Fiction." The Cresset, 36 (April, 1973),
    11-15. Meyer reviews several works here, including
    Museums and Women. The main concern of the essay

is to review City of Words by Tony Tanner; according
to Meyer it is "the best study of recent American
fiction yet written." Museums "reaffirms Updike's
position as one of America's major writers and
verifies his pre-eminence as a short story writer."

"Museums and Women and Other Stories." Publisher's Weekly,
202 (28 August 1972), 259. Short review which lists
both the regular and limited Knopf editions.

Prescott, Peter S. "Following Through, Sadly." Newsweek,
80 (23 October 1972), 106-109, 112. The problem with
Updike's novels, Prescott feels, is that "he
awkwardly sketches a realistic fabric over a lumpy
mythic structure"; this is not true with his short
stories. In Museums and Women, these stories, "unlike
his novels, exemplify the perfect marriage of
ambition to performance."

Rohrback, Peter T. "Museums and Women and Other Stories."
America, 127 (16 December 1972), 535-36. These
stories are concerned with fear: "this fear, seldom
expressed and infrequently considered, is the

eternal one of aging and eventually dying." Updike
"has chosen to give us this astonishingly accurate
portrait of one segment of our society as he sees
it."

Skow, John. "Sliding Seaward." Time, 100 (16 October 1972),
91. This review of Museums and Women begins rather
vaguely: "Is it Updike's faint tinge of smugness?
Is he too much a cherisher of clever conceits? The
reasons seem murkier the more they are examined, but
they refuse to be examined away." Skow believes
"The Hillies" and When Everyone Was Pregnant" are
"superb."

Tanner, Tony. "The Sorrow of Some Central Hollowness."
New York Times Book Review, 22 October 1972, pp. 5,
24. The people in Museums and Women seem incomplete
to Tanner: "What I seldom if every feel is that these
inhabitants of Tarbox or wherever have experienced
the capacity to love--as distinct from the inclina-
tion to copulate and the compulsion to propogate."
Since he did not like Rabbit Redux, Tanner feels that
"perhaps the shorter mode [as opposed to novels]
reveals Updike at his best."

Todd, Richard. "Updike and Barthelme: Disengagement."
Atlantic, 230 (December 1972), 126-32. While Todd
praises Updike's "detached voice" and his "celebrated,
lushly intricate descriptive style," he writes
wistfully of Museums and Women: "A certain moral
paralysis afflicts Updike's fiction (though it is a
problem from which Harry Angstrom tries to free himself in Rabbit Redux.) It becomes more visible now, as
Updike's shorter fiction loses its exact grip on the
present moment. The stories address themselves to a
cultural situation that held sway most strongly when
Updike began his career...."

Wood, Michael. "Great American Fragments." New York Review
of Books, 14 December 1972, pp. 12-18. Review of
several books including Museums and Women. Wood likes
three of the stories ("When Everyone Was Pregnant,"
"The Hillies," and "I Am Dying, Egypt, Dying"); in
the rest, "Updike wavers between very funny but very
lightweight pieces...and very pretentiously meaningful
ones like the title story."

Wyndham, Francis. "John Updike's Bulging Suitcases." The
Listener, 6 April 1972, p. 454. Wyndham objects to

the "clinical glamour" which Updike imparts to his
characters in <u>Museums and Women</u>. The readers merely
observe, rather than learn from, or share emotions
with, the characters. This results in a "sense of
strain."